Who Lives in…
THE MOUNTAINS?

Who Lives in...
THE
MOUNTAINS?

Ron Hirschi

Photographs by
Galen Burrell

A *WHERE ANIMALS LIVE* BOOK

G.P. Putnam's Sons   New York

Text copyright © 1989 by Ron Hirschi
Photographs copyright © 1989 by Galen Burrell
All rights reserved
No part of this book may be reproduced in any form
without permission in writing from the publisher.
Published simultaneously in Canada.
Printed in Hong Kong by South China Printing Company
Designed by Charlotte Staub

Library of Congress Cataloging-in-Publication Data
Hirschi, Ron. Who lives in—the mountains?/Ron
Hirschi; photographs by Galen Burrell. p. cm—(A Where
animals live book) Summary: A tiny bird in each
photograph leads the reader through the mountain forests
and streams to view the mountain goats, pikas, bluebirds,
and other animals that live in the high country.
1. Alpine fauna—Juvenile literature.   2. Alpine fauna
—United States—Juvenile literature.   [1. Alpine
animals.]   I. Burrell, Galen, ill.   II. Title.   III. Series.
QL113.H57 1989   591.52′64—dc19   87-25160 CIP AC
ISBN 0-399-21900-5
First impression

For Rosanne

High
above the
clouds, where the
wild paintbrush
grows,

snow-white goats
leap from rock to rock.

Their path leads to where
snow melting beneath a
silent ptarmigan
trickles into a
mountain stream.

Dippers
hop in and out
of the cold water as
the stream tumbles through
a marmot's meadow before
plunging to the valley,
far below.

Listen for
the marmot's whistle.
Can you hear its shrill,
"*Phweeee!*", echo in the distance?

Can you see
the mother pika
picking flowers?

She eats some
for breakfast and saves
some too—for the long
mountain winter
ahead.

Pikas scurry
through the
meadow...
while blue
grouse strut

and
weasels hunt
for mice

beneath
the watchful
eyes of a
junco

and
a mountain
bluebird.

Suddenly, the air turns cold.

An evening grosbeak
stops eating berries in its
favorite juniper tree.
Mule deer sniff
the air.

Do they
hear a black bear

or see
the bighorn sheep?

No!
They hear
thunder crash
as lightning flashes
and a flock of tiny birds,
rosy finches, flies
through the
darkened
sky.

The storm
passes quickly
and the rains wash
into the mountain stream.

It winds through the
chickadee's forest,

growing into
a river where
otters chase
dragonflies

and
moose take
a bath.

Here in the river valley,
elk and their calves

climb a summer path to the
high peaks above.

What will they see
and what will they hear
along their way to where
the wild paintbrush
grows?

AFTERWORD
for Parents and Teachers,
Big Brothers and Sisters

From a distance, mountains appear to be covered only with snow. A closer look reveals many animals living in meadows, in mountain forests, and along cold streams that tumble down from the high peaks.

Pikas, mountain goats, dippers, and ptarmigan are among the inhabitants of North American mountains. Pikas live only in high places where the air is cool, even in summer. Lower elevations and hotter temperatures would be fatal to their sensitive bodies; a summer of hay harvesting allows them to feed beneath winter's snow cover. Mountain goats have soft feet that help them cling to steep trails and their white fur blends well with the snow. Dippers plunge into mountain streams, flying underwater with outstretched wings in search of aquatic insects. Ptarmigan change color twice each year, molting from winter white to a darker, mottled feathering when paintbrush and other summer flowers bloom.

The alpine summer is brief but it is the best time to watch mountain animals. Each mountain has its own special features and no matter if you search for pikas and mountain goats in the Rockies and other western mountains, listen for the songbirds of the Great Smokies, or watch for playful river otters in the Adirondacks, you will see many birds and mammals in the high country. You will also see many changes as you climb to the highest peaks. Follow a mountain stream as it plunges from the melting snowfields. Listen for the song of the mountain chickadee. Smell the fragrant pines. And, watch closely for the blue grouse, weasel, deer, and other animals that call the mountain home.